The 30-Day Money Challenge

Building Stronger Habits, One Day at a Time

by

Tamra S. Connor, Ph.D.

Notes

This book is part of the TnT WayPoints Personal Finance series, created to help real people build real financial confidence through clarity, honesty, and daily action.

For permissions, inquiries, or educator resources, visit:
https://www.tamraconnor.com

First Edition

ISBN: 979-8-950867-00-2

Cover + Interior Design: TnT WayPoints Creative

Published by TnT Waypoints Publishing, USA

TnT Waypoints, LLC is committed to empowering individuals and educators with practical, accessible tools that build lifelong financial strength, one intentional step at a time.

Printed in the United States of America

Notes

Introduction

The Power of 30 Days

Money doesn't change because you hope it will.
Money changes because you change.
Not all at once
Not overnight

Not because you suddenly become a different person

It changes because you start making small, intentional decisions that add up over time.

That's what this challenge is about.

Thirty days is long enough to build momentum, but short enough to feel doable. It's a reset button, giving you a chance to get honest, get organized, and get moving toward the life you want.

You don't need perfection.
You need to make progress.

You don't need more money to start.
You need a starting point.

You don't need to know everything.
You need to take the next step.

This book gives you those steps.

Notes

How to Use This Book

Each day includes:

- A simple challenge
- A short lesson to help you understand the "why."
- Reflection prompts deepening your awareness
- An original inspirational quote to anchor the day

You can complete one challenge per day or stretch them out. What matters is consistency. This is your guide, your journal, your accountability partner, and your reset, all in one.

Let's begin!

Awareness

Turn on the lights. See the truth. Face the Numbers.

Days 1–10 focus on clarity, honesty, and understanding your current reality. Every transformation begins with a moment of honesty. The kind that's uncomfortable at first, but freeing once you let it in.

The Awareness Phase is that moment. It's where you turn on the lights and finally see your financial life clearly, without flinching, without hiding, without apologizing.

These first ten days aren't about fixing anything. They're about understanding everything.

Your habits
Your patterns
Your numbers
Your truth

Awareness isn't judgment. Awareness is power.

And once you see the truth, you can never unsee it, and that's exactly what makes this phase so life-changing. By the time you reach the end of Day 10, something inside you will have shifted. You've looked at your spending, your income, your credit, your habits — all the things you used to avoid. And instead of feeling overwhelmed, you feel . . . ***lighter***.

Awareness has a way of doing that. It clears the fog and quiets fear. Awareness gives you a starting point. Once you can see your financial life clearly, a new question arises.

A question you probably have not asked yourself in a long time:

What do I actually want?

And that question leads you forward.

DAY 1
Track Every Dollar Today

Every financial transformation starts with one simple truth: you can't change what you can't see. Today, you turn on the lights.

For me, it started on a Tuesday. It wasn't a dramatic Tuesday, nor was it a "my life is falling apart" Tuesday. No, it was just a regular, nothing-special, swipe-your-card-without-thinking Tuesday. I stopped to buy a breakfast sandwich and a coffee because I was hungry and tired while driving to work. When I got to work, I realized that in my rush to leave the house that Tuesday morning, I had left my lunch sitting in the fridge. I was busy and already thinking about everything I needed to do that day. At lunch, without thinking, I ran to the corner deli to grab a sandwich. By late afternoon, I wanted chocolate and a Dr. Pepper to perk me up before a long meeting. None of it felt like a decision. I was operating my day on autopilot.

But that night, scrolling through my bank app, the list of tiny transactions felt louder than usual, not really scary, but it was a little eye-opening to see that I had spent almost $50. $50 in one day on coffee, lunch, and chocolate. Everything that I had at home, but forgot to grab in my rush to get out the door, because I was tired.

Looking at my bank app, I realized something: I wasn't choosing where my money went. My habits were choosing for me.

I am sure you have been there too.

And today, that changes.

“Awareness is the first step toward control.
You can’t manage what you refuse to see.”

The Challenge

Write down every dollar you spend today. Every purchase. Every swipe. Every tap. No skipping.

Why This Matters

Most people don’t have a spending problem; they have an *awareness* problem. You can’t change what you can’t see. Tracking your spending is the financial equivalent of turning on the lights in a messy room. Suddenly, everything becomes clear.

Today isn’t about judgment. It’s about honesty.

Purchase	Amount	Purchase	Amount

Reflection

What surprised you about your spending today?

DAY 2
Check Your Account Balances

Avoidance keeps you stuck. Awareness sets you free. Today, you face your numbers with courage, not fear.

You woke up thinking about yesterday, not in a panicked way, but in a "something shifted" way. Awareness does that. It lingers. It taps you on the shoulder.

You hesitated before opening your banking app today. Your thumb hovered for a second longer than usual. But you opened it anyway. And as the numbers loaded, you felt a mix of relief, discomfort, and clarity. You experienced the emotional cocktail of someone finally facing the truth.

It wasn't as bad as you feared. It wasn't as good as you hoped. But it was real.

And real is where change begins.

"Numbers don't judge you.
They guide you, if you're willing to look."

The Challenge

Look at every account you have: checking, savings, credit cards, loans, apps, everything.

Why This Matters

Avoidance is expensive.

Clarity is free.

When you know your numbers, you make better decisions. When you avoid your numbers, you drift on autopilot, and drifting is how people end up stressed, overdrawn, or overwhelmed.

Today is about facing reality with courage.

Assets		Debts	
Account	**Balance**	**Account**	**Balance**

Reflection

How did you feel seeing the real numbers?

DAY 3

Calculate Your Monthly Income

Your income is the foundation of your financial life. Before you build anything, you need to know exactly what you're working with.

Today felt different. You sat down with your notebook or your phone, whatever you had, and for the first time in a long time, you weren't guessing. You weren't rounding. You weren't hoping the math would magically work itself out.

You listed your income, and as the numbers took shape, something clicked: You've been building your entire financial life on estimates. It's no wonder it felt shaky.

But as you wrote down your true monthly income, you felt a surprising sense of grounding. Like you were finally standing on a solid floor instead of financial quicksand.

You're not just looking at numbers anymore.

You're building a foundation.

"You can't build a strong financial future on guesses. Start with the truth."

The Challenge

List every income source and calculate your true monthly income.

Why This Matters

Your income is the foundation of your financial plan. If you don't know what's coming in, you can't make intentional decisions about what goes out.

This step is simple, but it's powerful.
It grounds you in reality and gives you a clear starting point.

Source of Income	Amount

Reflection

Does your income feel stable, flexible, or unpredictable? Why?

DAY 4

List Your Fixed Expenses

These are the non-negotiables. They are the bills that shape your monthly reality. Understanding them gives you control over the rest.

There's a strange kind of calm that comes from writing things down, even the things you'd rather ignore.

Today, as you list your fixed expenses, you notice something: these aren't just bills. They're the structure of your life.

Your home
Your transportation
Your commitments
Your responsibilities
The things that keep your world running

For the first time, instead of feeling weighed down by them, you feel grounded. These numbers aren't surprises. They're constant. And constants give you something to build on. You're starting to see your financial life not as chaos, but as a system you can understand.

Organization removes chaos.

"Clarity creates control.
When you know your numbers,
you reclaim your power."

The Challenge

Write down every fixed expense you pay each month. These are the bills that don't change.

Why This Matters

Fixed expenses are the backbone of your financial life. They're predictable, stable, and often non-negotiable. When you know this number, you know the minimum cost of your life, and that's powerful.

Most people underestimate their fixed expenses because they forget the "quiet bills" that auto-draft in the background.

Today is about bringing them into the light.

Fixed Expenses	Amount
Mortgage/Rent	
Car Payment	
Car Insurance	
Home Insurance	

Total Fixed Expenses	

Reflection

Which expenses are essential, and which ones could be renegotiated or reduced?

DAY 5

List Your Variable Expenses

This is where your habits live. They create your patterns and highlight your impulses. Variable expenses are your opportunities. Today, you get honest about them.

Variable expenses are where the truth hides, in the little choices, the emotional purchases, the "I'll deal with it later" moments. As you list them today, you feel a flicker of recognition. These numbers tell a story, too, but it's a different kind of story. Today's story is about habits, moods, convenience, and coping.

Do not judge yourself. Instead, notice the patterns. And noticing is powerful. It's the moment when unconscious spending becomes conscious awareness. It's the moment when you realize you're not just tracking money.

You're learning about yourself.

"Your habits tell the truth long
before your bank account does."

The Challenge

List the expenses that change from month to month. Include groceries, gas, eating out, shopping, entertainment, and everything in between.

Why This Matters

Variable expenses are where most people lose money without realizing it. These categories are flexible, which means they're also where overspending hides.

Today isn't about cutting anything. It's about understanding your patterns so you can make intentional choices.

Understanding leads to intention.

Variable Expenses	Amount
Groceries	
Electricity	
Water/Trash	
Gas/Propane	
Auto Fuel	

Total Variable Expenses	

Reflection

What surprised you about your variable spending? What changes can you make to reduce variable expenses?

DAY 6

Choose a Budgeting Method

A budget isn't a cage, but it is a compass. Today, you choose the system that will guide your next steps.

You've tried budgeting before, but it always felt like wearing someone else's shoes. Shoes that are stiff, uncomfortable, and not made for you. Today feels different. Today, you're choosing a method that fits your life, your personality, your rhythms.

As you read through the options, something clicks. You're not trying to force yourself into a system. You're choosing a system that supports you.

For the first time, budgeting feels less like restriction and more like alignment.

Your budget becomes your financial compass. It is one of the most important waypoints along your journey.

"The best budget isn't the fanciest one,
it's the one you'll use consistently."

The Challenge

Choose one budgeting method to use for the next 30 days:

- Zero-Based—Every dollar is assigned to an expense
- 50/30/20—50% of your income is allocated to your needs (fixed expenses and those variable expenses that must be paid); 30% of your income is allocated to your wants; and 20% is allocated to savings and debt payments.
- Envelope—You place a specific sum of money into an envelope (paper or digital). Each envelope represents one of your fixed or variable expenses, and once the envelope is empty, you cannot spend any more on that category.
- Hybrid—A combination of two or more budget models.

Why This Matters

A budget is not a punishment; it's a plan. The right plan depends on your personality, lifestyle, and goals.

You don't need the "perfect" method. You need the one you'll actually stick with.

This is about alignment, not aesthetics.

Reflection

Why does this method fit your life right now?

DAY 7
Build a Simple Weekly Budget

Weekly planning keeps you grounded. It's where intention meets real life, one week at a time.

There's something refreshing about planning just one week.

Not a whole month
Not a whole year
Just seven days

It feels doable, manageable, and human.

As you sketch out your weekly budget, you feel a quiet confidence growing. You're not trying to predict the future. You're preparing for it. You're not trying to control everything, just the next few steps.

And that's enough. In fact, it is more than enough.

It's progress.

"Small weekly plans prevent
big monthly problems."

The Challenge

Create a one-week spending plan based on your income and expenses. If you are paid bi-weekly or semi-monthly, create a spending plan for the period of time between your paychecks, if you prefer.

Why This Matters

Monthly budgets are great, but weekly budgets are practical. They keep you grounded, flexible, and aware of what's happening right now, and not 30 days from now.

Weekly budgeting helps you course-correct quickly, rather than waiting until the end of the month to realize you overspent.

Reflection

What feels realistic for this week?

DAY 8
Review Your Subscriptions

Tiny leaks drain big goals. Today, you plug holes and reclaim your money.

You didn't expect today to feel emotional, but it does. As you scroll through your subscriptions, you see the ghosts of past seasons. You see the workout app you swore you'd use, the streaming service you forgot you had, the free trial that quietly became a monthly bill. Each one is a tiny reminder of a moment when you meant well but didn't follow through.

But instead of feeling guilty, you feel . . . ready. Ready to release what no longer serves you. Ready to stop paying for things you don't use. Ready to reclaim the money you didn't even realize you were losing.

Canceling a subscription may feel small.

Today, you reclaim your power.

"Every dollar you reclaim is a dollar you can redirect toward your goals."

The Challenge

List every subscription you pay for, including streaming, apps, memberships, and renewals. Now cancel at least one.

Why This Matters

Subscriptions are the silent budget killers. They're designed to be forgotten. Companies count on you not to notice and keep paying month after month.

Canceling one subscription won't change your life, but the mindset shift will.

Subscription	Amount
Netflix	
Hulu	
Uber One	
Gym Membership	

Total Subscriptions	

Reflection

Which subscription was easiest to cancel? Which one surprised you?

DAY 9

Check Your Credit Score

Your credit score is a snapshot of your financial habits. Today, you look at it with clarity, not judgment.

— — —

You check your credit score with the same energy you'd use to peek through your fingers during a scary movie, with a little curiosity, caution, and while slightly braced for impact. But when the number appears, something surprising happens and you don't spiral. You don't judge yourself. You don't compare. You just . . . observe.

It's a number, not a verdict. A simple snapshot, not your final destiny. And for the first time, you see it as information. Not as your identity.

You're learning to separate your worth from your wallet.

"Knowledge is leverage. The more you know, the better decisions you make."

The Challenge

Look up your current credit score.

Why This Matters

Your credit score is a financial passport. It affects your interest rates, insurance premiums, housing options, and sometimes even job opportunities.

Knowing your score isn't about judgment, but it is about awareness.

You can't improve what you don't acknowledge.

Reflection

What's helping your score? What's hurting it?

DAY 10
Review Your Credit Report

Your credit report tells your financial story. Today, you read it with fresh eyes and full ownership.

Your credit report reads like a timeline of your life, the apartment you moved into when everything felt new, the credit card you opened during a stressful season, the loan you took when you needed help. Some entries make you smile. Others make you wince.

But as you read, you realize something important: You've survived every chapter.

Your past decisions do not define you. You're informed by them.

And today, you're choosing to write the next chapter with intention.

Big changes begin with a first step.

"Your credit report is a story,
and you have the power to edit it."

The Challenge

Read your full credit report from all three bureaus.

Why This Matters

Credit reports contain errors more often than people realize, and those errors can cost you money. Reviewing your report is an act of financial self-protection.

This is your chance to correct mistakes, catch fraud, and understand the story your credit history is telling.

It is your chance to take the necessary steps to rewrite your future.

Reflection

Did anything surprise you or need correction?

Awareness to Alignment

Awareness asks you to look honestly at where you are, not where you meant to be or where you think you "should" be. Awareness is just your truth of right now. Awareness of your habits, your patterns, and your money story as it actually shows up in your daily life.

By now, you've seen things you used to overlook. You've named expenses you forgot you were carrying. You've noticed choices that help you and choices that quietly drain you. That clarity is your first real turning point. Because once you see your financial life clearly, you can finally decide what deserves to stay, and that's where you're headed next.

Alignment is the moment you stop reacting and start choosing. It's where you take everything you've noticed, including the helpful, the messy, the surprising, and begin sorting it against the life you actually want. Awareness shows you the map. Alignment helps you choose the direction.

Reflection

What truth about your current financial habits feels most important to carry with you into Alignment? And how might it shape the choices you make next?

Alignment

Decide what matters. Choose your direction.

Days 11 – 17 shift from awareness to intention. Setting goals, choosing strategies, and aligning actions with values become your focus for the week.

Awareness showed you the truth. Alignment is about deciding what to do with it.

This is the phase where you stop letting your habits run the show and start choosing what actually fits the life you want to build. Alignment isn't about perfection or overnight change. It's about making sure your money, your values, and your daily decisions are all aligned.

You've already uncovered what's been working for you, and what hasn't worked. Now you get to sort through it with intention. What deserves to stay? What needs to shift? What no longer matches who you are becoming?

Alignment is the moment you take ownership of your path. It's where clarity becomes direction on your journey to financial wellness.

Let's start shaping your next steps with purpose.

By Day 17, you will have done something powerful.

You've chosen. You've named your goals. You've identified your patterns. You've set your direction. And with that clarity comes a new kind of energy, the kind that makes you want to move.

You're no longer wandering. You're walking with purpose. And now that you know where you're going, it's time to take the steps that will get you there.

This is where the work begins, not the heavy kind, but the steady kind. The kind that builds momentum. The kind of work that builds confidence.

The kind that changes your life.

Notes

DAY 11

Calculate Your Total Debt

Debt feels heavy until you name it. Today, you take back your power by facing the full picture.

There's a moment, right before you total the numbers, when your stomach tightens. You already know the debt exists. You've felt it in the background like a low hum. But seeing the full amount on paper feels like turning toward a shadow you've avoided.

And yet, when the number finally stares back at you, something unexpected happens. It is a sense of relief. Because now you know. Now it's real. Now it's something you can work with.

The unknown was heavier than the truth.

"Debt is loud in your mind until
you quiet it with a plan."

The Challenge

List every debt you owe, including credit cards, loans, medical bills, and personal loans, everything. Now, calculate the total.

Why This Matters

Debt feels overwhelming when it's foggy. But when you put it on paper, it becomes a plan. Seeing the full number can be uncomfortable, but discomfort is often the doorway to change.

Debt loses its power the moment you face it.

Debt	Amount	Interest Rate

Total Debt		

Reflection

How did it feel to see your total debt in one place?

DAY 12

Choose a Payoff Strategy

Momentum or math, either will work. Today, you choose the strategy that keeps you moving forward.

You look at your debt list again, this time with a different energy. You're no longer standing at the base of a mountain wondering how to climb it. You're choosing your path, not with dread, but with strategy.

Snowball

Avalanche

Motivation

Math

There's no wrong answer. Pick the strategy that keeps you moving.

Today, you stop reacting to your debt and start directing it.

"A plan turns fear into focus."

The Challenge

Choose one strategy to guide your debt payoff

- Snowball (smallest balance first)
- Avalanche (highest interest first)

Why This Matters

A strategy gives you direction. It turns random payments into intentional progress. Snowball builds motivation. Avalanche saves money. Neither is wrong, and the best method is the one you'll stick with.

How the Debt Payoff Strategies Work

Snowball Strategy

Core idea: You pay off debts from **the smallest balance to the largest balance**, no matter the interest rate.

How it works:

- Make minimum payments on all debts.
- Put every extra dollar toward the **smallest** debt.
- When that debt is gone, roll its old payment into the next-smallest debt.
- Repeat until all debts are eliminated.

Avalanche Strategy

Core idea: You pay off debts from **the highest interest rate to the lowest interest rate**, regardless of balance.

How it works:

- Make minimum payments on all debts.
- Put every extra dollar toward the highest-interest debt.
- When that debt is gone, roll its old payment into the next-highest-interest debt.
- Repeat until all debts are eliminated.

Debt	Amount	Interest Rate	Priority

Reflection

Why does this strategy motivate you?

DAY 13

Set a Mini Emergency Fund Goal

Security starts small. Today, you build the first layer of your financial safety net.

You think about the last time an unexpected expense knocked the wind out of you, maybe you are remembering that car repair, the medical bill, or the broken appliance. You remember the stress, the scrambling, the feeling of being one surprise away from chaos.

Today, you decide you're done living like that.

A mini emergency fund isn't glamorous, but it's powerful. It's a promise to your future self: "I've got you."

And that promise feels like peace.

"Security isn't built in a day.
It's built one intentional dollar at a time."

The Challenge

Choose a starter emergency fund goal, typically $500 to $1,000, and commit to building it over the next three months.

Why This Matters

A mini emergency fund protects you from life's small surprises, so they don't become big setbacks. This is your financial shock absorber.

It is your first line of defense.

Reflection

What would having this cushion change for you?

DAY 14
Have a No-Spend Day

Today, you pause the spending autopilot and reconnect with what you truly need.

Today, you notice how often you reach for your wallet without thinking, out of habit, boredom, convenience, or emotion. You catch yourself mid-scroll on an online store. You pause before grabbing a snack you don't really want. You walk past a display that would've tempted you last week.

It's not about deprivation. It's about awareness.

And with every "not today,"
you feel a little stronger.

"Discipline is choosing what you want most over what you want now."

The Challenge

Spend nothing today. No extras. No impulse buys. No, "it's only $5."

Why This Matters

A no-spend day resets your habits. It shows you how often you reach for convenience, comfort, or distraction.

It's not about deprivation
it's about awareness.

Reflection

What did you avoid spending today?

DAY 15
Review Your Spending Patterns

Your patterns reveal your priorities, even the ones you didn't mean to set. Today, you learn from them.

Looking back at your spending the last two weeks feels like reading a diary you didn't know you were keeping. The patterns are subtle but honest. Those late-night purchases, the stress-relief snacks, the convenience meals on busy days reveal a pattern of financial decisions.

But instead of judging yourself, you feel curious. You're starting to understand the "why" behind your spending, not just the "what."

And that understanding is the beginning of real change.

"Your money follows your habits.
Change the habit, change the outcome."

The Challenge

Look back at your spending from the last two weeks and identify patterns.

Why This Matters

Patterns reveal priorities, even the ones you didn't mean to set. This step helps you understand your habits so you can shape them intentionally.

Reflection

What patterns stood out to you?

DAY 16
Create a Savings Goal

A clear goal gives your money direction. Today, you choose a destination worth working toward.

There's a moment today when you pause, really pause, and ask yourself what you want. Not what you "should" save for. Not what other people say matters. What *you* want.

A goal that feels:

Personal

Meaningful

Yours

As you write it down, something shifts. This isn't just about money anymore. It's about direction. It's about choosing a future that excites you instead of one that just happens to you.

For the first time, saving feels less like a sacrifice and more like self-respect.

"A clear goal gives your money direction
and your effort purpose."

The Challenge

Choose one savings goal and set a deadline.

Why This Matters

A goal without a timeline is a wish. A timeline turns your goal into a commitment.

Whether it's travel, a purchase, a sinking fund, or a dream, naming it gives it power.

Reflection

Why does this goal matter to you?

DAY 17

Automate One Thing

Automation is your silent teammate. Today, you let automation remove some of the mental load.

You've spent weeks making conscious decisions, and today you give yourself a gift: one less thing to think about. You automate a bill, a transfer, or a payment, and it feels like setting a boundary with chaos.

It's a quiet kind of relief. A relief because knowing that even on your busiest, most distracted days, something in your financial life is still moving forward.

You're building systems that support the person you're becoming.

You are becoming the person you want to be.

"Automation is discipline on autopilot."

The Challenge

Automate one financial task: a bill, a savings transfer, or a debt payment.

Why This Matters

Automation removes decision fatigue. It protects you from forgetfulness, stress, and inconsistency.

When you automate your priorities, you guarantee your progress.

Reflection

How will this automation reduce the mental load stress?

Alignment Spurs Action

Alignment is where your financial life stops drifting and starts pointing in the direction you actually want to go. In this phase, you took everything you uncovered in Awareness—your habits, your numbers, your patterns—and held it up against your values and long-term goals. Alignment asks one honest question:

Does the way you use your money reflect the life you say you want?

This section helped you identify what's supporting your future and what's quietly working against it. You clarified your non-negotiables, defined what "enough" looks like, and chose the behaviors that match the person you're becoming. When your spending, saving, and earning line up with your purpose, money stops feeling chaotic and starts feeling intentional.

And that's the point: Alignment sets the stage for Action. Once you know what matters and what needs to shift, the next step is to build the systems, habits, and strategies that turn your aligned intentions into daily movement. Action becomes easier, not because life gets simpler, but because your direction finally makes sense.

Reflection

Which part of your current financial life feels most out of alignment with the person you want to be, and what's one small shift that would bring it closer to your values?

Action

Build the habits. Do the work. Create momentum.

In Days 18–25, you will start implementing systems, making changes, and taking tangible steps.

This is the phase where clarity becomes movement.

You've seen your truth. You've chosen your direction. Now you begin building the habits, systems, and structures that support the life you want.

Action isn't about doing everything at once. It's about doing the next right thing, consistently, intentionally, and with a sense of purpose.

These days are practical
Tangible
Empowering

You're not just learning anymore. You're becoming.

By Day 25, you will have taken real steps, not theoretical ones, not "someday" ones, but actual, meaningful action steps. You've made decisions. You've built systems. You've created momentum.

And with momentum comes something new: awareness of what's working and what isn't.

You start to notice the habits that feel natural and the ones that still feel heavy. You see the progress you've made and the places where you still need support.

This is the moment when action evolves into refinement.

DAY 18

Review Your Insurance Coverage

Insurance isn't exciting, but it's essential. Today, you make sure your protection matches your reality.

Insurance has always felt like background noise, something you pay for but rarely think about. But today, as you read through your policies, you realize how much of your life is protected by these quiet little contracts.

You see gaps you didn't notice before. Strengths you didn't appreciate. And for the first time, you understand that insurance isn't about fear. It's about preparation.

You're learning to protect your future with the same care you're using to rebuild your present.

"Protection is a form of preparation, and preparation builds confidence."

The Challenge

Review your health, auto, renters/home, life and any other insurance policies.

Why This Matters

Insurance isn't exciting, but it's essential. It protects your financial stability when life throws the unexpected at you.

Today is about making sure you're covered. That you are not overpaying, and not under-protected.

You are developing a much-needed risk management plan.

Type of Coverage	Insurance Company/ Agent	Coverage	Exclusions	Premium	Deductible	Policy Limits
Home						
Auto						
Life						
Health						
Disability						

Reflection

What did you learn about your coverage? What should you change?

DAY 19
Identify One Money Leak

Leaks hide in habits. Today, find one and fix it.

You spot it almost immediately, that one small habit that's been quietly draining your money. Maybe it's a fee. Maybe it's a convenience. Maybe it's a crutch. Maybe it's a vice you have been wanting to eliminate from your life. Maybe it's a pattern you didn't realize had become routine.

But instead of feeling frustrated, you feel empowered. Because now you see it. And once you see a leak, you can fix it.

Today, you tighten one bolt on the ship you're learning to steer.

"Small leaks sink big ships.
Patch them early."

The Challenge

Find one recurring money leak. It can be something small that adds up, and then fix it.

Why This Matters

Money leaks are sneaky. They hide in habits, fees, convenience, and autopay. Fixing even one leak creates immediate breathing room.

Reflection

What leak did you find, and how will you fix it?

DAY 20
Create a Sinking Fund

Future expenses don't have to be surprises. Today, you can plan ahead to reduce tomorrow's stress.

You think about the expenses that always seem to catch you off guard. It could be the holidays, the car repairs, the school fees, or the trips you want to take. They're not surprises. They're just unplanned.

Today, you change that.

You choose one future expense and start preparing for it. And suddenly, the future feels less like a storm you must brace for and more like a destination you're planning toward.

You are building your life plan.

"Planning ahead turns
chaos into calm."

The Challenge

Choose one upcoming expense and start a sinking fund for it. Determine how much you need to set aside, each payday, so you are ready when the expense is due.

Why This Matters

A sinking fund turns future stress into future readiness. It prevents "emergencies" that aren't emergencies, just unplanned events.

Reflection

What sinking fund did you choose, and why?

DAY 21

Review Your Paycheck Deductions

Your paycheck tells a story most people never read. Today, you learn exactly where your money goes.

You look at your paycheck with new eyes today. Not just the final number, but the path your money takes before it reaches you. Taxes, benefits, insurance, and retirement are the hidden architecture of your financial life.

For the first time, you understand where your money goes and why. And that understanding feels like stepping into a room you've walked past for years but never entered.

You're learning the language of your own income.

"When you understand your paycheck,
you understand your power."

The Challenge

Look at your paycheck and identify every deduction, including taxes, insurance, retirement, benefits, everything.

Why This Matters

Your paycheck is a roadmap. Most people only look at the final number, but the real story is in the deductions. Understanding where your money goes before it hits your bank account gives you clarity, control, and confidence.

This is about knowing the
***true* value of your work.**

Reflection

What did you learn about your paycheck, deductions, and net pay?

____

____

____

____

____

____

DAY 22

Set a 1-Year Financial Goal

A year is long enough to change your life. Today, you choose the goal that will lead the way.

You sit with this one a little longer. A year can change your life, but it's still close enough to feel real. You think about what would make the biggest difference. What would make future-you breathe easier, stand taller, and feel proud?

When you finally write down your one-year goal, it feels bold. A little scary. But also, exciting.

You're not just reacting to life anymore.
You're designing it.

"A year from now, you'll wish you had started today. So start."

The Challenge

Choose one meaningful financial goal you want to accomplish in the next 12 months.

Why This Matters

A one-year goal gives you direction. It's far enough away to be ambitious, but close enough to feel real. This is your chance to choose something that excites you, challenges you, and moves your life forward.

Reflection

What is your one-year goal, and why does it matter?

DAY 23
Declutter Something and Sell It

Your home holds hidden value. Today, you turn clutter into cash and clarity.

You pick up an item you haven't used in months, maybe years, and you realize it's been taking up space in your home and your mind. Letting it go feels like exhaling. You feel more organized and ready to continue growing on this journey.

When you sell it, the cash is nice. But the clarity is better. You're learning that your environment and your finances are connected, and that releasing what you don't need makes room for what you do.

Today feels like a reset, inside and out.

"Letting go of what you don't
need makes room for what you do."

The Challenge

Choose one item you no longer need and sell it online, to a friend, or at a resale shop.

Why This Matters

Decluttering creates space, mentally, physically, and financially. Selling something reminds you that your home is full of value you've already paid for. Turning unused items into cash is a small but powerful win.

Reflection

What did you sell, and how did it feel to let it go?

DAY 24

Review Your Banking Setup

Your bank should support your goals, not slow them down. Today, you evaluate your tools.

You've spent weeks learning the truth about your habits, your numbers, your patterns. Today, you turn your attention to the tools that hold your money. As you look at your accounts, fees, and features, you realize something you've never fully acknowledged: you deserve better than "whatever bank you happened to open an account with years ago."

You deserve tools that support your goals. Tools that make your life easier. Tools that match the person you're becoming.

Today, you stop settling for default settings and start choosing with intention.

“The right tools make the journey easier.
Choose wisely.”

The Challenge

Evaluate your bank accounts, fees, interest rates, and features.

Why This Matters

Your bank should work for you, not drain you with fees or limit your options. Today is about ensuring your financial tools align with your financial goals.

Reflection

What changes do you want to make to your banking setup?

DAY 25

Identify Your Money Strengths

You're doing more right than you realize. Today, you acknowledge the habits that are already working.

You've spent so much of your life focusing on what you need to fix that you almost forget to notice what you're doing right. But today, as you list your strengths, something warm rises in your chest. It may be pride or recognition that you have grown and are taking steps to preserve your own financial wellness.

You see the moments you made smart choices. The times you stretched a dollar. The discipline you didn't give yourself credit for. The resilience you didn't realize counted.

You're not starting from scratch.
You're starting from strength.

"Your strengths are proof that you're capable of more than you think."

The Challenge

List the things you do well with money, even the small things.

Why This Matters

Most people focus on their mistakes and overlook their strengths. But confidence grows when you acknowledge what you're already doing right. Strengths are the foundation you build on.

Reflection

What are your top money strengths?

Action Allows for Adjustment

Action is where your financial life stops living on paper and starts showing up in real time. In this phase, you took the clarity you built in Alignment and turned it into movement by taking small, consistent, repeatable steps to reshape your habits, your systems, and ultimately your outcomes. Action isn't about perfection or intensity; it's about building a rhythm you can actually sustain.

This section helped you translate aligned intentions into daily behaviors: setting up automations, creating spending boundaries that align with your values, choosing priorities, and practicing the discipline of doing the next right thing, even when it's inconvenient. Action is where confidence grows, not because everything goes smoothly, but because you learn you can follow through.

And that's the truth most people miss: taking action doesn't guarantee a straight line. Life shifts. Income changes. Emergencies happen. Motivation dips. That's why the next phase, Adjustment, is essential. Once you've been in motion long enough to see what's working and what's not, Adjustment gives you the space to refine, recalibrate, and realign without shame. It's where your plan becomes resilient instead of rigid.

Reflection

What is one action you've taken recently that moved you closer to the life you want, and what did it teach you about what needs to be adjusted next?

____

____

____

Adjustment

Refine

Strengthen

Sustain

Become the next version of yourself.

In this final phase, you will evaluate, adjust, and prepare for long-term success. Adjustment is where growth becomes identity.

This phase isn't about starting over; it's about fine-tuning. It's where you look honestly and compassionately at your strengths, weaknesses, wins, and challenges. It's where you refine your habits, reinforce your progress, and prepare for long-term success.

Adjustment is the phase that turns a 30-day challenge into a lifelong shift.

It's where you step into the next version of yourself. The one you've been building since Day 1.

When you reach Day 30, you will realize something profound: You didn't just complete a challenge. You changed your relationship with money and with yourself.

You're more aware

More aligned

More capable

More confident

And the best part? This isn't the end. It's the beginning of a new chapter, one you now have the clarity, tools, and confidence to write with intention.

Your journey continues from here.

DAY 26
Identify Your Money Weaknesses

Weaknesses aren't failures. They're opportunities. Today, you name them so you can change them.

Naming your weaknesses feels different now. They are no longer heavy or shameful; they are just honest. You've built enough awareness and confidence to look at your habits without flinching.

You see the patterns that trip you up. The emotional triggers. The blind spots. The places where old versions of you still linger.

But instead of feeling defeated, you feel empowered. Because now you understand them.

And what you understand, you can change.

"Awareness turns weakness into wisdom."

The Challenge

Name the habits that hold you back. All of them, including overspending, avoidance, impulse buying, lack of planning, everything.

Why This Matters

Weaknesses aren't failures. They're opportunities. When you name them, you take away their power. When you understand them, you can change them.

Reflection

What weakness are you ready to work on first?

DAY 27

Create a Future-You Vision

Your future self is waiting. Today, you imagine the life you're building and the person you're becoming.

You close your eyes and picture the version of yourself with steady habits, calm confidence, and a financial life that feels aligned rather than chaotic. You imagine peace, stability, and freedom. Today, for the first time, it doesn't feel like a fantasy; it feels like a direction.

You've spent 26 days learning who you've been. Today, you imagine who you're becoming.

And that vision becomes your compass.

> "Your future self is waiting
> for you to show up."

The Challenge

Write a vision of your financially confident future self. Describe the life you want, the habits you've built, and the peace you feel.

Why This Matters

Your vision becomes your compass. When you know who you're becoming, your daily decisions start aligning with that version of you.

Reflection

What does your future-you look like, feel like, and live like?

DAY 28
Do a 10-Minute Financial Cleanup

Small tasks create big clarity. Today, you tidy up one corner of your financial world.

"Small steps create big clarity."

The Challenge

You tackle one tiny task today. A task that is something so small it almost feels insignificant. But as you tidy that corner of your financial world, you feel a surprising sense of clarity. It's like wiping a smudge off a mirror and suddenly seeing yourself more clearly.

You realize that progress isn't always loud. Sometimes it's quiet. Sometimes it's simple. Sometimes it's ten minutes.

But it counts. It all counts.

Spend 10 minutes cleaning up something small, deleting old emails, organizing receipts, renaming files, updating passwords, or tidying your financial space.

Why This Matters

Small maintenance prevents big messes. Ten minutes may not feel like much, but it builds momentum and reduces stress.

Reflection

What did you clean up today?

DAY 29
Celebrate a Win

Progress deserves recognition. Today, you celebrate the effort, the growth, and the momentum.

You look back at the last four weeks and feel something you didn't expect: pride. Not because everything is perfect, but because it isn't. Not because you did everything flawlessly, but because you didn't. Celebrate because you showed up, **again and again**.

Even on the days you didn't want to.

You've built awareness.

You've built habits.

You've built momentum.

Today, you let yourself feel the win.

"Every win counts.
Celebrate the progress, not the perfection."

The Challenge

Choose one win from this month. It can be big or small. Now, you need to celebrate it.

Why This Matters

Celebration reinforces progress. It reminds your brain that effort leads to reward. This is how habits stick.

Reflection

What win are you celebrating today? How are you celebrating?

DAY 30

Build Your Next 30-Day Plan

This isn't the end; it's the launchpad.

Today, you choose what comes next.

You have reached the final day, but it doesn't feel like an ending. It feels like a beginning, and it is. Today, you can start a new chapter shaped by clarity, intention, and confidence. You're not the same person who started this journey.

You're steadier

More aware

More capable

More in control

You choose one habit to carry forward. One milestone to pursue next. One commitment to honor.

And as you write it down, you realize something powerful: You didn't just complete a challenge. You changed your relationship with money — and with yourself.

"The journey doesn't end here.
This is your new beginning."

The Challenge

Choose one habit you want to continue and one milestone you want to reach in the next 30 days.

Why This Matters

Financial growth is a cycle, not a finish line. Today marks the end of this challenge and the beginning of your next chapter.

Reflection

What habit will you continue? What milestone will you pursue next?

Adjustment is where your financial plan becomes a living system instead of a fixed set of rules. After taking action long enough to see real patterns, you now see what's working, what's draining you, and what's surprising you. You have given yourself a great gift, permission to refine without guilt. You have permitted yourself to achieve financial wellness. This challenge was not about starting over; it was about responding to reality with clarity instead of emotion.

In this section, you learned to evaluate your habits, spending, priorities, and systems with honesty and curiosity. You identified friction points, celebrated what's sticking, and made targeted tweaks that keep your plan aligned with your values and your current season of life. Adjustment teaches you that progress isn't linear, and it doesn't need to be. What matters is your ability to pivot with intention rather than react out of frustration or shame.

And as you move forward, Achievement helps you recognize the milestones you've reached, the identity you've grown into, and the long-term stability you've built through every cycle of awareness, alignment, action, and adjustment.

FINAL REFLECTION

Your Money Story Is Changing

You've spent 30 days showing up for yourself. Thirty days choosing awareness over avoidance. Thirty days building habits that support the life you want.

This challenge wasn't about perfection. It was about progress, and you made it.

Now you know your numbers. You understand your habits. You've built momentum. You've proven to yourself that you can do hard things.

Your financial story is still being written, and you're writing it with more clarity, confidence, and intention than ever before.

Your future self is already grateful.

Reflection

As you think back on the past 30 days, what feels different? Not just the numbers, but also your mindset. How will you keep that momentum alive beyond these 30 day?

The Next Journey

You've just completed 30 days of showing up for your money, your mindset, and your future. That alone puts you in rare company. Most people talk about wanting change; you actually practiced it. You built awareness, aligned your choices with your values, took action that matched your season, and learned to adjust with intention instead of shame. That's real growth.

But this challenge was never meant to be a finish line. It was a doorway.

This book is the first in a growing series of TnT Waypoints Challenges. Each challenge is designed to help you strengthen a different part of your financial life with the same grounded, honest, no-fluff approach you've experienced here. Think of this as your foundation. From here, you'll move into focused 30-day journeys that help you build skills, confidence, and clarity one step at a time.

Upcoming challenges in the series will guide you through topics like:

- 30 Days to Better Budgeting: Building a Spending Plan That Actually Fits Your Real Life
- 30 Days to Debt Confidence: Understanding, Organizing, and Tackling Debt Without Shame
- 30 Days to Savings Momentum: Creating Systems That Make Saving Automatic and Sustainable
- 30 Days to Smarter Spending: Reshaping Habits, Triggers, and Patterns So Your Money Supports Your Values
- 30 Days to Financial Resilience: Preparing for Emergencies, Uncertainty, and Life's Inevitable Curveballs

Each challenge stands alone, but together they form a full roadmap—a series of waypoints that help you build a financial life that feels stable, intentional, and yours.

You've proven you can commit. You've proven you can grow. Now you get to choose your next waypoint.

Your journey continues from here.

www.ingramcontent.com/pod-product-compliance
Lightning Source LLC
LaVergne TN
LVHW040516210926
848480LV00005BA/1475